Contents

If you are interested in other aspects of real estate my other books will serve you well.

Wholesaling Real Estate: A beginners Guide

Rental Property Investing for the Rest of Us: The Beginners Guide to Successful Rental Property Investing

Becoming a Real Estate Agent: A Comprehensive Guide on How to Become a Real Estate Agent

Chapter 1

What is Property Flipping?

Have you heard about it? Have you watched TV programs about it? Property flipping – it seems to be all the rage. But what really is flipping real estate all about?

> *Definition:*
> *Property flipping is generally defined as buying and selling a home in the same calendar year.*

More often than not, however, flipping real estate involves repair and/or renovation in order to realize a profit on the resale of the home.

There are two basic methods to making money flipping homes:

The Quick Flip

An investor locates a home that is substantially below market. He purchases the home. He then may opt to fix a few minor items, apply a fresh coat of paint or simply update the visual appeal of the home. He then quickly resells it at market value.

The Renovation

In this scenario, the investor locates a home that is in need of substantial repairs, modernization, or rehabilitation. The home is purchased and over the period of several months, it is renovated to maximize the market value. The investor realizes a profit after subtracting the original purchase price and all repairs and selling costs from the sales price.

How Money is Made Flipping Homes

Sounds easy enough, right? Well, yes and no. There is a lot of money to be made flipping houses, but unless it's done correctly, there is a lot of money to be lost.

- *A flipper must know the pulse of the market*. They need to understand what buyers demand in the marketplace and what they are willing to pay for.

    The investor pays $125,000 for a home and spends $25,000 renovating the kitchen but buyers will only pay $10,000 - the investor just lost $15,000.

- *An investor must be able to accurately price repairs*. It can be a real challenge to accurately project renovation costs. Even experienced contractors freely admit that you do not know the extent of a renovation job until you get into it.

    The investors budgets $10,000 to renovate the kitchen, only to find out that the subfloor is rotten and all the wiring is below electrical standards. The total cost was $15,500. The buyer will only pay $10,000 for the kitchen - the investor just lost $5,500.

✒ *The investor needs to accurately estimate the After Repair Value (ARV) before beginning the rehab.* The success of property flipping almost entirely relies on the resale value. The amount and quality of the renovation hinges on this number.

> *The agent calculates that the $125,000 home will sell for $165,000 after spending $25,000 in renovation and paying for closing costs, earning the investor $15,000. The agent over-estimated the value and the property's true market value was only $148,000. The investor lost all his profit and paid $2,000 out of pocket.*

The success of flipping homes relies on certain variables, which if incorrectly calculated could turn a money making venture into a financially crushing loss.

Can You Really Make Money Flipping Houses?

The answer is yes but a qualified yes. You need to know what you are doing. You need to know how to study the market, how to know what buyers want, how to measure the profitability of a project and then turn around and sell it.

Although property flipping is not as active as it was during the recent foreclosure process, there is still a solid market for this niche. According to RealtyTrac, home flips made up only 4.5 percent of sales during the second quarter of 2015 but the return on investment has jumped from 24 percent to nearly 36 percent over the past year.

How this Book Will Help

This book is going to show you how to master each step of the house flipping process. In addition, we will address these additional areas:

✒ *What kind of properties make good flips*

✒ *Where to locate these properties*

- *How to evaluate the feasibility of a property*

- *How to purchase the home*

- *How to find financing*

- *What repairs bring the best return*

- *and much more...*

Before we jump into inspections, calculating costs and determining profitability, we are going to show you how to prepare for your first flip. Let's start with building your network and then we will move on to how understanding your market will help you choose the right property.

Chapter 2

Creating Your Network

In order to successfully flip a property, you are going to need a team of experienced professionals. Before you begin analyzing deals, submitting offers and grabbing your hammer, take the time to set up your network first. This will help ensure your success.

Licensed Real Estate Agent

One of your first steps will be to locate a qualified real estate agent. Whether you decide to buy property from their Multiple Listing Service (MLS) or not, they will be a vital member of your network. A real estate agent will provide you with the following helpful services:

Submitting Offers to Purchase

Real estate agents are trained negotiators. Their purchase agreements are designed to legally protect you the purchaser. In addition, they will prepare, submit and track the offer for you freeing up your valuable time.

Plus, your buyer's agent is free! Agents receive payment through the seller's commission. So if you are making an offer on a MLS listing, why not use an agent that is working *in your behalf* rather than putting the offer through the agent that is working for the buyer (and not you).

Presenting CMAs

Do you have the time, the training and the resources to record, track and measure all the properties that have sold in your market area over the past 12 months? Probably not. But your agent has them all stored in a nice neat database and they would be more than happy to prepare a Comparative Market Analysis (CMA) for you.

The purpose of a CMA is to determine the most likely sales price of a property by comparing (and adjusting) recent similar sales in the neighborhood. When you combine the agent's experience and knowledge of the market along with this data, you have an invaluable resource to make sure that you are not paying too much for a property.

Determining Your ARV

What is an ARV you ask? It stands for the "After Renovation Value" or "After Repair Value." In effect, it is the most likely sales price of your property after you have repaired, remodeled or renovated it. This is *the critical* number upon which all your estimates, calculations and profits will be based on. You do not want to take a guess. You definitely do not want to be wrong. Having a professional who can prepare that number with accuracy is absolutely worth it.

Locate Buyers

Real estate agents who have been in the business for many years will have a large network of buyers and contacts.

How to choose a good real estate salesperson?

Not all salespeople are the same. Some are little better than a used car salesman and others have been in the business so long that they are a trusted professional that even appraisers admire (and that is saying a lot). Here are a few tips to help with the interview process:

- *Use only agents that work in the business full-time.*

- *Look for someone who has been in the business for at least 5 years.*

- *How many transactions (buying or selling) did they complete last year?*

- *Would they be willing to complete CMAs and ARVs on properties you are interested in purchasing?*

- *Check with a few past clients. If they were satisfied then probably you will be too.*

If the agent will charge you for completing a CMA or ARV, do not act shocked or offended. They have no doubt met many fly-by-night "investors" that only wasted their time. Assure them that you would only ask for their advice and opinions on properties that you are seriously considering – and then be willing to pay their fee (which is generally around $100).

Licensed Contractors

Unless you have a contractor's license and plenty of skills and experience in rehabbing houses, you are going to need a contractor. Not only will they be used for some, if not all, of the project, but their initial inspection of the property and their comments about it will be critical to your evaluation.

You will likely need several different contractors to do different parts of the job. For right now, concentrate on getting a general contractor in your network. They will no doubt be able to recommend others as you need them. Your real estate agent will also know of others who have good and honest reputations.

How to Find a Good Contractor

When you are renovating a house, the job needs to be done right – the first time. A buyer is going to demand quality construction. The quality of the work will have a direct correlation to the sales price of the property.

That being said, stay away from the handyman type contractors. These are the guys that generally do work on the side. Often they are not licensed or insured. Though they may be cheaper, it will show in their work and if something goes wrong, you will have little recourse.

Instead, look for licensed, bonded and insured builders or general contractors that have years of experience in their field. Ask for a list of testimonials and phone numbers of some recent clients and check to see if they were satisfied with the work. Also check with their clients on the ability to keep a reasonable timetable.

How to Get the Best Quality of Work from Your Contractor

One of the easiest way to ensure that your contractor completes everything that you have in mind is to get all bids in writing and then pay attention to the detail. If the contractor says he will paint the exterior, find out if the price includes pressure washing. Will it cover painting the doors and trim and all outbuildings? Getting these details in writing will save you and the contractor a ton of stress.

Home Inspector

Buyers nearly always opt to hire a home inspector to look over the property before they waive their purchase contingencies. Though you cannot recommend that they use your inspector, having one as part of your network will come in handy – for two reasons.

The Purchase Property Inspection

Though you will have a contractor as part of your team, a property inspector can come in handy as well. If you are looking at a quick flip or a home that appears to only need superficial improvement, a general contractor may not be necessary – but a complete inspection is. This is a good time to bring in the home inspector. They are going to carefully examine the property and look for things that you could easily miss.

The Pre-Sales Inspection

Imagine the expression on the buyer's face when they receive their inspector's report on your property with a list of 25 items. You know they are a list of nit-picky things that have no real effect on safety or value, but now the seller is insisting that your property is not worth your asking price and the deal falls through.

I would have saved you a world of trouble by getting an inspection completed *before* you list the home for sale. In this way, you can take care of everything that the inspector finds. When your buyer receives the report from his inspector, he will be surprised to see a home in pristine condition.

How to Choose a Home Inspector

You want an inspector that is both thorough and trustworthy. Here are a few questions you will want to know the answer to before he joins your team:

- *Are you licensed or a member of a home inspector association?* In many states, you do not have to be licensed to be a home inspector. Inspectors who are members of either ASHI (American Society of Home Inspectors) or NAHI (National Association of Home Inspectors) must adhere to a code of ethics and demonstrate expertise and competency.

- *Do you have a contractor's license?* Locate a home inspector that either is or was a general contractor. They will have a much better grasp of construction techniques, problems and building codes.

- *How long have you been a home inspector?* It takes many years of experience and training to develop the skills and insight needed to be a good home inspector.

Do you carry Errors and Omissions (E&O) Insurance? If the inspector misses a major problem, their E&O insurance can help you to recover your damages. Never hire an inspector that does not have this type of insurance.

Real Estate Appraiser

Usually an appraiser is only hired when a buyer is getting bank financing and it is the lender that hires the appraiser. However, there will be projects that are so complex that you will want more than just a CMA from your agent.

> *Take for example a 2 bedroom/1 bath property purchased for $150,000. The market demand is for a 3 bedroom/2.5 bath property that includes a master suite. You anticipate that the construction of the master suite plus remodeling the kitchen and replacing the roof will cost $125,000. Before attempting the construction, getting an ARV appraisal will help you to make sure you can make money off the project.*

Real estate appraisers are the experts in valuation. They apply a broader range of value tests than real estate agents. They have a greater degree of technical knowledge and are also required to have E&O insurance. They can make a nice addition to your team – even if they are only used occasionally.

Lender

This maybe stating the obvious, but it needs stating. If you are going to start flipping homes full-time, you are going to need a good working relationship with a lender or two.

I have found in my experience, that it is much easier to build a good working relationship with small community banks and local credit unions, rather than the big national chains who do not like short-term loans. Community banks and credit unions have less stringent loan criteria and they are much more open to short-term loans. In addition portfolio loans that are offered by

Developing a Working Relationship with Your Agent

I want to take a moment to discuss an important issue. We will soon start talking a lot about gathering market data to make a purchase decision. You will quickly realize how having a real estate agent on your team is going to help you.

That is why I want to take just a minute to discuss how to build a good relationship with your agent.

You never want to give your agent the impression that you are just using them to get market data with no intention of actually using them in a transaction. Real estate wholesalers are notorious for doing this and it is has left a really sour taste in the mouths of a lot of agents.

Remember, every time you buy a property using your agent, it is the seller that pays them – not you. So get rid of the notion that this agent is going to cost you money.

Now, when it comes time to sell, if you list the property with your agent then yes you will need to pay them commission. However, if you loyally use the same agent every time you purchase a property through the MLS, I doubt they will mind if you only use them on the buying side of the equation.

If you really want to motivate your agent to bend over backwards for you and put in that little extra work that will make your CMA's even more accurate, then give them as many referrals as possible. The more experience you get, the more contacts you will develop. Pass them along local lenders, you may want to look into hard money or private investor loans.

This can also be a good time to explore your finance options. Property flippers generally average 6 months until they turn around and sell the property. You will want to begin looking into how you will finance your purchase and building a relationship with these sources in order to expedite future purchases. We will discuss finance options in greater detail in Chapter 4.

Title Company

When it comes to handling a closing, I personally prefer using a title company rather than an attorney. For one, they are cheaper. Their in-house attorneys can quickly put together your paperwork and they will charge much less.

Title companies are also useful when you want to complete a title search on a property. This comes in handy when you are researching abandoned homes, properties in foreclosure or properties that have multiple owners in common.

From time to time, you might find such a good deal that you could flip the property instantaneously to another buyer and walk away with some quick cash. Having a title company that is willing to handle a simultaneous or double close can be a challenge to find, so ask around as the need arises. Putting together your network or team is important. You can do this before you start or as you begin working on your first property. Feel free to ask for recommendations from your friends, colleagues and other real estate professionals.

Chapter 3

This chapter is less about how to identify a specific property and more about studying national trends, finding the right neighborhood, and identifying buyers. It doesn't make any sense to start fixing up a property to what you like, if your tastes do not reflect market demands. Flipping is all about meeting a buyer's needs and wants.

How the National Economy Affects Flipping

Remember the housing crisis from 2007 to 2010? It did not start in all areas all at once. Alan Greenspan, former Chairman of the Federal Reserve revealed that the United States was not experiencing a nationwide housing bubble per se, but a number of local bubbles. In 2007 he was quoted in saying that "all the froth bubbles add up to an aggregate bubble" Investors who watched the national housing market could see what was appearing on the horizon and be prepared for it before it hit their neighborhood.

Mortgage Interest Rates

National mortgage interest rates have a direct correlation to real estate buying and selling. Low interest rates encourage first time home buyers to move out of renting and into home ownership. It can also motivate some home owners to upgrade their way of life by moving to a larger or more luxurious home.

On the other hand, if you begin to notice steadily rising interest rates, you can anticipate a decrease or slowing in real estate activity. This could affect the number of willing buyers for your property.

Lending Requirements

Since the housing crisis, the federal government has cracked down on risky, interest only loans to sub-prime borrowers. Keeping abreast of current lending requirements can help you to focus your renovations and marketing to groups that are most likely to qualify for a mortgage. On the other hand, tighter mortgage guidelines also open the door for owner financing which is a great way to maximize your return.

Unemployment Rates

The unemployment rate is a reliable gauge to measure the health of the national economy. The lower unemployment is, the more jobs that are available and the more money there is in the market place to be spent. A rise in unemployment is never a good thing and could forecast a longer marketing time on your properties.

Know Your Market Area

While it is important to watch national employment trends, variations in interest rates and mortgage terms and other economic indicators, real estate is more of a local phenomenon. It is critical to have your finger on the pulse of your local housing market. Without knowing what is going on locally, you are shooting blind and risking tens or even hundreds of thousands of dollars in the process.

Local Economic Stability and Growth

Part of understanding your market area is understanding the local economy. This means that you need to know what is going on in the Planning and Zoning office. Watch for announcements of new developments or proposed construction (residential, developmental, commercial or even industrial). This will help you so see where the market is going.

For example, if you attend the monthly public planning and zoning meeting and find out that they have approved a large shopping mall to be built on the outskirts of town, you now know where buyers are going to be looking to live. Why not get a jump on the game and start looking to purchase fixer-uppers within 5 miles of that development.

On the other hand, if you read in the local paper that one of the major area employers is having financial problems and is starting to lay off employees, how will this affect residents? Will they feel like their jobs are secure? If not, do you really see them buying a home soon? Perhaps this is the time to being studying other market areas or looking into cheaper homes.

Local Real Estate Activity

This is where your real estate agent is going to be an important member of your team. Yes, you could setup a spreadsheet and spend the time to track all the data yourself, or, you could measure what you know against someone who is in that market day in and day out.

Before showing up in your agent's office with the question, "Can you tell me what is going on in the local housing market?" why not email him or her a specific list of questions and areas that you want to learn about. This will give them time to look over the data and provide you with concrete evidence rather than their personal perceptions.

Here are some questions that you need to find the answers to:

 What percentage of listed homes are REO's? What percentage of a discount do these properties usually receive? Buying REOs (bank repossessions) can get you a property that is below market value, but not all the time. Buying property from a bank can be a lengthy process. They are notorious for selling property "As Is" and hate to lower the price if a problem is found. These properties often come with a limit on how quick you can resell the property. If REO's are being discounted less than 10%, expand your focus to traditionally listed homes – you will have a lot less hassle.

- *How much are average homes selling for?* If 60% of the homes sold over the past 12 months were between $145,000 and $175,000, you should not expect to find a home for $50,000 and then turn around and sell it for $200,000.

- *What is the average days on market for the main price categories?* This is a great number to keep your eyes on. It measures demand in the market for certain types of homes. It also indicates how long it will take to sell your property. This is helpful in figuring out your holding costs.

- *What types of properties are selling the quickest?* If your agent can narrow down which are the fastest selling homes, you will be able to measure what buyers want. Do these homes all have similar features, layouts or sizes? Are they all in the same general area/neighborhood?

- *What neighborhoods have the most activity?* You personally may like a certain area in town, but if typical buyers are looking elsewhere, you are going to need to put your personal preferences aside and focus on the areas of town with the most action.

Who is Your Buyer?

You could renovate a home once a month for a year, but unless you can sell those homes, you will quickly go broke. So, before you even start looking for properties to flip, you must first understand who your buyer is and what they are looking for.

I would recommend that you offer to buy your agent lunch to discuss this particular topic. You want to know where the market activity is coming from.

- *Are buyers young families, working professionals or retirees?*

- *What neighborhoods appeal to which buying groups?*

- *Are buyers paying cash or getting mortgages? Are they getting traditional mortgages are more interested in owner financing?*

- *What type of home is each buying category interested in?*

What Buyers Want

Once you learn who in your area is buying, now you need to narrow down what they are looking for. If you can create homes that meet the top needs of buyers and then throw in a couple of wants, you will be able to demand a competitive price and may even get multiple offers.

I have combined my personal experience along with a detailed national study of what buyers are demanding in the market place. Here is a list of the top 10 wants and needs:

1. **Updated Kitchen and Baths** - Young buyers want a new kitchen and because many have put most of their savings into the down payment and furnishings they lack capital to complete it themselves. New bath fixtures are an important feature and dramatically increase the appeal.

2. **Open Eat-In Kitchen** - Scratch formal dining rooms and open up the kitchen. The kitchen has become the hangout room for families and entertaining. Eat-In kitchens are especially in demand with families with children.

3. Exterior Lighting – Focus on wall lanterns, ground spotlights and landscape accent lights. These make an attractive first impression and enhance curb appeal.

4. Separate Laundry Room – Buyers see a separate laundry room with an area for ironing and folding clothes as a huge benefit. A recent study states that 93% of buyers want this feature.

5. Open Floor Plan – Buyers favor an open floor plan rather than a layout that compartmentalizes the home.

6. Home Office – Young buyers are more likely to work at home than older generations. A home office is important for them.

7. Walk-In Pantries – A recent study stated that nearly 85% of buyers would prefer a walk-in pantry that also has room to store mops and brooms.

8. Low Maintenance Turn Key Homes – Buyers want homes that need little to no work. This is especially important when it comes to landscaping and flooring. Wood

floors and granite countertops are good options.

9. Wireless Services – Young buyers could care less about landlines. Purchase homes that provide good internet access and service. Consider installing a wireless home security system which ranks the highest among technology features buyers would like to have.

10. Energy Efficiency – Young buyers are going green and are energy conscience. It is not a top seller, nor are a lot of buyers willing to spend more for these features, but if you are going to upgrade the appliances or replace the furnace or windows, make sure they are Energy Star rated.

What Buyers Hate

While buyers do have some personal preferences, across the board there are some features that will turn them off completely. If you purchase a home that has these factors, I would recommend you change them out – regardless of their condition.

1. Popcorn Finished Ceilings - That is so 1980's, scrape it off and give them a smooth ceiling.

2. Brass Fixtures - Think grandma's house. Buyers are looking for a more modern appeal.

3. Vanity Strip Bathroom Lighting - They don't want to be blinded or feel like they are an actor getting ready in some cheap back stage theatre.

4. Lack of Storage - They don't really care where the storage is (basement, garage, or attic) but it is a real turn off if a home is lacking it. A few well-placed shelves and built-in cabinets can quickly fix that problem.

5. Tight Homes - Buyers hate homes with small compartmentalized rooms, they want an open floor plan. Before busting out walls, however, get a skilled contractor and an architect in there to make sure you won't be removing load bearing walls.

Location is a Factor

In addition to amenities within the home itself, the location of the home will play a factor. Talk to your agent to determine if buyers in your areas prefer the suburbs or downtown.

If you will be marketing to families, make sure your properties are in a safe area close to schools and parks. Many buyers prefer homes that are close to public transportation and that have a good walk score. Other amenities such as close proximity to dining, shopping, recreation and entertainment can be a plus.

A great area to focus on is neighborhoods that are undergoing rejuvenation – either by others fixing up their homes or through direct investment by the city. Areas with commercial expansion indicate a possible influx of residential occupants in the near future.

Now that you have narrowed down your market and your buyer, it is time to take the results and start looking for a property to purchase. In the next chapter, we will break down each step of the process.

Chapter 4

Getting Financing

If life were a dream, we would all have enough cash under our mattress to buy a house and pay for its renovation. But unfortunately, that is only a fantasy for those starting out in the business. So, we are going to analyze a couple of ways you could get funding to purchase and renovate your fix-and-flip.

Obtaining conventional financing as a multi-property buy-and-hold investor can be a challenge on its own, but getting conventional short-term financing is near to impossible. Property flippers typically are looking at financing that will extend no more than 12 months with a target of less than six.

National lenders make their money on their ability to sell loans to the secondary mortgage market. Fannie Mae and Freddie Mac are only interested in long-term loans. Thus, to obtain conventional financing, you will need to find a lender that will hold the loans in house.

Conventional Financing

Obtaining conventional financing is perhaps the "safest" way to pay for a property flip – besides paying cash. In-house loans are going to be backed, not by the Federal government, but by the equity in the home and your personal credit worthiness. A good place to start shopping around is to visit local banks and credit unions. They often write short-term portfolio loans.

In order to qualify for these types of loans, you are going to need to meet stricter lending requirements and will most likely need a larger down payment. You must have a good credit score for starters. You should shoot for a score of 620 or above. You will get a lower interest rate if you are in the 700s.

When looking for a lender, go meet with several. Be upfront with them about what you plan to do and how you will go about it and how long you expect the loan will be active. Be prepared to share your real estate experience and/or a list of qualified team members. Work to become pre-qualified. This will help you narrow down your property choices and speed up the closing process.

If you decide to go conventional, make sure that your loan does not have a prepayment penalty. Many conventional loans also carry a restriction on when you can resell the property. There can be some really hefty penalties for a violation, so watch out!

Hard Money Loans

Hard money loans (HML) are short-term, non-bank loans that are made by a company or private investor. The loan is guaranteed more by the property and less on the credit of the borrower. Hard money loans are used by savvy investors all the time. It is a tried and true way to finance a fix-and-flip.

When you know exactly what you are getting into and factor in the higher-than-average loan costs into your formula, it can be a great resource. If, however, you do not honestly weigh the risks, it can be a deal breaker. Why?

Hard money loans can be extremely expensive and need to be carefully factored into your profitability calculations. These lenders charge extremely high interest rates (14 -20%), carry multiple points (up to 10) and have high closing costs. Points are paid upfront with each point equaling 1% of the loan amount. But, they are perfect for short term loans.

The loans are usually made off the After Repair Value (ARV) and have a loan-to-value ratio of between 55% and 75% based on the borrower's credit score. This can pick up any purchase equity (unlike conventional mortgages) *and* include funding for repairs. Notice how it works in the following comparison:

Purchase Price	$100,000
Market Value	$120,000
ARV	$175,000

	Conventional Loan	Hard Money Loan
Loan	80% of Purchase Price	70% of ARV
Loan Amount	$80,000	$122,500
Down Payment	20% of Purchase or	10-20% of Purchase or
	$20,000	$10,000 - $20,000

Use a HELOC

Do you have equity sitting in your personal residence or in another investment property? If so, then consider accessing this equity through a Home Equity Line of Credit (HELOC). A HELOC is superior to an Equity Loan because the loan amount is more like a credit card limit than a bank loan. You can borrow up to the maximum loan amount, pay it back and then borrow again without having to go through the lending process each time.

These loans will only allow a maximum total loan-to-value of 80% which will include your first mortgage and the HELOC.

For example, if your home is worth $250,000 and you have a mortgage on it for $145,000. The maximum you *could pull out using a HELOC would be $55,000 ($250,000 x .80 = $200,000 - $145,000 = $55,000). This can be a great way to finance repairs on a property.*

The interest rate is higher than a conventional mortgage but the closing costs are less. But... if you are borrowing against your personal residence and the deal goes sour, make sure you have the monthly income to cover the additional loan payment.

Owner Financing

Buying a property on a land contract (also known as owner financing) can be a great way to finance a short-term purchase. Many property owners wouldn't mind making a little extra on the sale of their home. It can be a real win-win situation.

Instead of getting a mortgage, you would make monthly payments to the owner. A down payment is made at the time of closing which is generally less than 10%. The owner will charge interest which is usually one or two percentage points above conventional mortgage rates (perhaps higher because of the short term nature of the loan). When you are ready to resell the property, the remainder of the loan balance is paid to the original owner and you keep the profit.

This is a good option if you are lacking financing for a down payment. The owner could carry a mortgage on the property in the second position with the conventional financing being in the first. You would need to figure out, though, how to pay for the repairs.

Another option to use owner financing is to purchase the property "Subject To" the existing mortgage. The buyer pays the seller the difference between the purchase price and the mortgage balance. He then takes over the payments to the seller's mortgage. Though most mortgages contain a "due on sales clause," many lenders simply overlook this as long as the payment is made on time.

Most homeowners, however, do not like this option because they take a risk that the buyer – you – will not make the payments on time and hence trash their credit. Sellers who are quick to take this offer are usually ones that are already behind in their mortgage payments and are facing foreclosure.

Borrow from an IRA

We have talked about accessing your own home's equity or getting a hard money loan from a private investor, but did you know that you can finance real estate with either a self-directed IRA or a 401(k)? You can use your personal account or that of a private investor.

In order to use a retirement account to fund real estate, the IRA must be a custodial account. The repayment terms and payment schedule needs to be in writing and all payments, including the interest, would go back into the IRA. The beautiful part is that since IRAs are tax-exempt, the loan is either tax-free or tax-deferred based on the IRA type.

You should consult with an experienced advisor before trying to set this up since there are some very specific rules and regulations governing property purchases.

Getting Prepared

Since your loan is going to be based not only on your credit worthiness but also on the ROI on the investment, you are going to want to show a lender – regardless of who they are – that you know what you are doing and are aware of the costs and risks.

Once you have decided on your type of financing and hopefully gotten pre-qualified or at least pre-approved, you will no doubt need more evidence to finalize the loan. This will include a copy of the purchase agreement, contract with your contractor, multiple estimates of renovation costs, a marketing plan, anticipated holding costs and the projected time to completion.

You will need to be prepared to answer some hard questions such as:

- *How much experience do you have on such projects?*

- *How much of your personal funds are you using for this project?*

- *What happens if the construction costs are more than you estimated?*

- *What is your fall back or exit plan if the house does not sell in time?*

- *Would you be able to qualify for a conventional mortgage if the property does not sell?*

Chapter 5

How to Choose Property to Flip

Have you ever bought a piece of technology only to find out that you wish you had bought a different brand or model? If only you had done just a little more research, perhaps you would be a lot more satisfied. You try to be happy with your new purchase, but there is that persistent nagging doubt of whether you made the right choice.

Investing in real estate – whether to own it or flip it - is much the same. I don't want you to jump at the first property you find. Take your time. Analyze as many properties as you can find. Even if you only make an offer on one out of every 20, 30 or 40 properties. Wouldn't it be much smarter to invest in a property that you *know* is going to give you a return rather than one where you *think* might earn you a couple of dollars?

That being said, we have now reached the point where we start to discuss how to choose a property. There are a number of factors that must be analyzed and there are some pretty hard and fast rules that must be followed if you want to realize a profit.

Buying a house that will be flipped for a quick sale is much different than buying a house for your family. Buying your homestead is filled with emotion, visions and dreams. Investment properties are all about the bottom line – making you money. *You must check your emotions at the door. Do not get attached to a property.* If a potential investment fails to meet any of the qualifications, then you have to walk away – espe-

cially since you are just starting out. Getting emotionally in-
volved with an investment is a really quick way to divorce yourself from your money and future profits.

The Three Essential Rules

Remember how we talked about not getting emotionally attached? Well a great way to set yourself some boundaries is to
apply these three essential rules - even before you go and inspect the property for the first time. Before you even take the
chance of getting hooked by peeking at the property, see if it
meets these guidelines.

Test #1 – It Must Meet Buyer Requirements

You have spent a lot of time analyzing your market and
have found out what buyers in your market area want
and need. Do you have a checklist of must haves and
wants? If so, compare it to the property under analysis.

PROPERTY ANALYSIS CHECKLIST

Subject Property Address:

_____

List Price: __$110,000_____   DOM: _____   Date:
_____

Above Ground GLA: __1,100 SF__   Bedrooms: __3__   Baths:
__2__

Buyer Checklist

Needs	Subject Property (Comments)
3BR/2BA	☐
1,400 - 2,200 SF	☐
Energy Efficient	☐
2 Car Garage	☐
30 Minute Commute	☐

Physically check off the list as you go along. Your check-list might look something like this:

If this property met all your buyer's qualifications, then there would be no reason to fix-and-flip unless it was seriously below market. So do not expect the property to be perfect, but see if there is the *potential* to meet your buyer's needs. If it has the potential to meet your buyer's criteria, keep the property and move on to Rule #2. If it does not, discard it and move on to another property. Here are a few examples of the though process:

🔨 *Typical buyers are demanding 3BR/2 BA homes with between 1,400 and 2,000 square feet.* The subject property features 2 BR/1.5 BA and contains 1,400 square feet above grade. What does this tell you?

Either the bedrooms are exceptionally large or there are additional non-sleeping rooms such as a den or dining room. If that is the case, they could be easily converted into a bedroom thereby increasing the value and the market appeal of the property. Keep the property, move on to Rule #2.

🔨 *Typical buyers require that a home offers a 2 car garage.* The subject property meets size and layout requirements but there is no garage. So, you build one. But is it possible?

A quick analysis of the assessor's card indicates that the lot is narrow and the home nearly butts up to both of the side property lines. There is not even enough space to put a driveway to the backyard and build the garage there; nor is there room in the front of the house. Discard the property, move on to another.

🔨 *Buyers prefer properties within a 30 minute drive from major employment centers.* This 1960's property could easily be remodeled to meet all other buyer criteria but it is 45 minutes outside of town on an unpaved road with poor cell service.

If you create the most fabulous house and price it well but fail to meet the locational demand of buyers, your holding time (the amount of time it takes to find a buyer who doesn't mind living in the sticks) could eat up a large portion of your profit margin. Discard the property, move on to another.

If you want your property flipping business to succeed, you have to set firm unbreakable rules. Making sure that the property will be *quickly* marketable to your typical buyer is significant. This is not an area where you want to take risks. There will be enough risks to thrill you down the road - don't worry. Trust me, do not bend the rules on this first step.

At this point, you should have a detailed have and have not list. If it has passed Test #1, then move on to Test #2.

Test #2a – What is the True Market Value?
*This test is for quick flips - properties
that need little if any repairs.*

If you want to help reduce risk and increase the profit for property, you want to buy properties that are below market value. In an active real estate market where most properties are listed by agents, this can be a challenge. If you are negotiating a private purchase, then you will want to make sure they are not asking too much.

This is where your real estate agent and your own familiarity with the market will come in to play. The more experience you gain the easier it will be to realize if a property is listed below, at or above true market value.

At this stage in the game, you are simply wanting to "pre-qualify" the property. While studying the market either you or your agent should have access to a database of all recent sales.

Do a search of all sales within 12 months that have similar features such as construction type, size (± 20%), age (± 10 years), bedrooms, baths, basements, garages and land area. Once you have this, you can run the average and the median values off the sales prices (not list prices).

> *Let's say there were 23 properties and the average sales price was $102,000 and the median was $110,000.*

A more detailed analysis would be to calculate each sale to the sales price per above grade square foot ($85,000 sales price ÷ 900 sq. ft = $94.44). You would need to calculate this for each property and then take an average or median and then multiply that rate by the subject property.

> *If our subject property is 1,100 square feet and the average price per square foot was $94.44 then a possible sales price would be $103,900.*

Take these figures and compare it to the listing price. What is the average list price discount rate according to your agent? Multiply it to the subject property.

> *If the average discount rate was 5%, your formula would look like $110,000 list price x .95 = $104,500.*

The results would look like this:

PROPERTY ANALYSIS CHECKLIST

Subject Property Address: _____

List Price: _$110,000____DOM: _____ Date: _____

Above Ground GLA: _1,100 SF_ Bedrooms: __3__ Baths: _2___

Market Value Checklist

Number of Comparable Sales within 12 months? _23__

Average Sales Price: _$102,000_ Range -5% _$96,900_ +5%_$107,100_

Median Sales Price: _$110,000_ Range -5% _$104,500_ +5%_$115,500_

Price per Sq. Foot: _____$94.44_____ X _____Subject Proper-ty: _$103,900_

List Price Discount Rate: __5%____

Subject Property Discounted List Price: _$104,500_

It is important to understand that this is a very rough estimate of the possible market value. There have been no adjustments to the comparables for superior or inferior characteristics. This is just a general guide.

To help you not get hung up on one number, take your average and median sales prices and create a range of plus and minus 5 percent. Does the price per square foot calculation for the subject property fall within the ranges? How about the Subject Property Discounted List Price?

From the above analysis, the subject property is priced at the lower end of the value range – perfect for an investor like yourself. Now the key is to offer less than market value to realize your profit.

If the property was priced higher, you may have to prepare yourself for a buyer that wants full market value. Paying market value, however, does not eliminate the property from your analysis – that is if you are intending to alter the market value through renovation. But the cheaper you can get the property at the start the better. This moves us on to the test for renovation properties.

Test #2b – The 70% Rule

This test is for fix-and-flips - properties that need renovation and/or substantial repairs.

Property flippers swear by this rule. As long as you can accurately estimate the repairs, this rule is a tried and true way to make sure you make a nice 20% profit. Here is the formula:

$$(ARV \times .70) - Rehab\ Costs = Maximum\ Allowable\ Offer$$

ARV = After Repair Value: What the property will sell for when you are finished with all renovations and repairs. Your real estate agent will help you determine this number.

.70 = Profit + Soft Costs: This accounts for holding costs, mortgage interest, loan fees, unanticipated expenses and other soft costs and approximately a 20% investor profit margin.

Rehab Costs = Hard Costs: All costs for repairs are in this figure including permits, disposal, contractors etc.

Maximum Allowable Offer =   This is the price you will
                            offer
Purchase Price: to the seller.

Now, the question in your mind is how will you know what repairs need to be completed and how much they cost without doing a physical inspection and getting contractor estimates? Good question. Remember, however, this is simply the pre-qualification phase. This is to help you get a feel for the profit potential.

How though do you know what needs to be done? Look back at the pictures of the listing that your agent sent you or if it is an unlisted property, pull the assessors records or check and see if it was listed for sale within the past 5 years. Check out the pictures.

- *How is the kitchen? Is it dated?*

- *How many baths does it have to bedrooms?*

- *Can you tell the type and condition of the floor coverings?*

- *How does the outside look? Landscaping? Siding? Roof?*

- *Do the agent's comments reveal any details such as recent remodeling, "a handyman special," or that it was a rental?*

You can learn a lot from photos (especially online ones that can be enlarged). As you gain experience, you will be able to quickly estimate the typical repair costs for these items. Meanwhile, a quick call to your contractor for some general estimates will get the ball rolling. You will iron out the details down the road.

So let us go back to our worksheet and see what we can

PROPERTY ANALYSIS CHECKLIST

Subject Property Address: _____

List Price: _$110,000____ DOM: _____ Date: _____

Above Ground GLA: _1,100 SF_ Bedrooms: __3__ Baths: _2___

After Repair Value (AVR) _$162,000_   X .70 = _$ 113,400_

Renovation and Purchase Price Calculation

Room	Work	Price
Kitchen	Renovation	$ 15,000
Bath	Update	$ 2,500
Flooring	Replace Carpet	$ 8,000
Siding	Paint	$ 4,500
Hardware & Fixtures	Replace	$ 1,000

Less Total Renovation Costs   _$ 31,000_

Maximum Allowable Offer _$ 82,400_

Discount Off List Price   _25%___

learn:

If after the inspection, no other repairs would be needed, the maximum allowable offer (MAO) would be
$82,400. That represents a 25 percent discount off the
listing price whereas the market discount averages 5%.
What is the likelihood that the seller would accept your
offer? That takes us to Test #3.

Before we move on to Test #3, however, I want to mention that
though a 30% discount of the ARV is the sweet spot, there are
many markets that just do not allow for such a strong return. If
you find that after submitting 50 offers, none have been accepted, it is very possible that the market will not accept such

a high discount. If that is the case, resubmit your offers at 25%, but do not go lower than 20% or you risk putting in a ton of hard work and earning minimum wage for your efforts. If that doesn't work, then I bet you have forgotten to factor in Test #3.

Test #3 – What is the Seller's Motivation?

You can run computations and calculations day in and day out and find the absolute best deals, but unless a seller accepts your offer, you are doing little more than exercising your brain.

The motivation of the seller is a significant factor. Take our sample property for example. The property is listed for $110,000. You want to offer him 25% less than his list price.

- *What if the property was listed within the past 30 days?* Your chance of getting your offer accepted is about as likely as winning the lottery – slim to none. There is no reason why a seller would want to accept your low ball offer when he has just placed the property on the market.

- *What if the property has been sitting on the market for 120 days?* Now the motivation is changing. We know the list price is reasonable. We also know that the seller must be frustrated and anxious to sell. This is a good time to bring your offer to the table.

- *What if you find out the property has a recorded Notice of Default?* Now you are seeing real motivation. We have a seller with a house that won't move and if it doesn't sell soon, the bank will take it and he will be out everything. There is a good possibility that he would seriously consider your offer and gladly take extra 20 percent discount. He may even consider a Sub-

THE UN-RELIABILITY OF ZILLOW AND TRULIA

When calculating the ARV, stay away from public sites like Zillow and Trulia. These sites can give you a general estimate – like what you are working on at this point, but they are no way accurate enough to base a purchase offer on their data.

In 2012, Redfin conducted a study of the reliability of Trulia and Zillow. Their report stated that these two sites are missing around 20% of the active listings and that it takes 7 to 9 days before a new listing is uploaded. Additionally, 36.5% of their active listings are no longer for sale.

What does this actually mean? In active markets, not seeing a listing for 9 days could very well mean that great deal is already gone. What you are looking at are the mid-to-high priced homes that have no wholesale potential. On top of that, 35% of your time is wasted because you are researching listings that no longer exist. And if that wasn't bad enough, for every 80 homes you considered, you missed seeing 20 possibilities.

How about estimating property value? Zillow can provide you with a free estimate. But how accurate is their estimate? According to Zillow's own Zestimate data accuracy report, they have a median error rate of 8.3%. In fact, further down in their report they state that only 38.4 percent of the time are they within 5% of the actual sales price.

In the property flipping business, a 20% mistake in pricing is suicidal. Follow the Zestimate's price recommendations and you could very well lose all your profit on every deal. You need to base any purchase decision on actual verified comps along with active listings from the local MLS.

ject To sale if you can catch up the payments as part of your down payment.

If you want to make the best use of your time, start with the oldest active MLS listings first and then work up. This way you will have the most discouraged sellers and hence the most motivated at the top of your list. Also, focus your attention on non-listed sellers that have received NODs or are going through other time-sensitive life changing events such as divorce or a job move.

The motivation of the seller is a huge factor in determining whether or not to present your offer now or to wait a while and let them get a little more desperate.

These three tests are non-negotiable.

If you start changing these variables to make a property "work," then you run the risk of seriously jeopardizing your ability to gain a profit off the investment. It is better to be patient and wait for a good investment opportunity than to rush in and lose $10,000 of your own money in the deal.

Chapter 6

How to Purchase a Property to Flip

This chapter is going to breakdown the process of actually purchasing the property – from the offer to the inspection and all the way to the closing. Buying a fixer-upper is nearly the same process as buying your personal residence, but we want to share with you a couple of tricks of the trade that will protect you.

The Purchase Agreement

There are two basic types of properties that you will be purchasing – the properties that are listed with a licensed agent (in the MLS) and those that are not (FSBOs). For Sale by Owner (FSBO) properties can be a little more of a challenge because you do not have anyone in your corner advocating your rights. But basically the processes are the same. In fact, I recommend you use the same purchase agreement.

For your first couple of transactions, it is a good idea to work along with your real estate agent to find listed properties. Though the discounting may not be as great, the buying process carries less risk and your agent will help you become intimately familiar with the buying process.

Real estate agents have their own purchase agreements. Once you locate a property, they will fill out the form for you and submit it to the buyer's agent. If you decide to step out and make your own offers on non-listed properties, copy that same form and use it for your offers. Just remove statements that link the form to any real estate companies, agents or licensing authorities. Since these are state mandated forms, all the legal protection clauses are in there. No sense reinventing the wheel.

Purchase Price

As we have previously discussed, you will want to pay the lowest possible price, but in some markets, properties are selling at or even above the list price. In that case, it can be almost impossible to get a buyer to consider a discounted offer.

Do not give up, just change your strategy. You can always make a full price offer and then renegotiate for a lower price after your inspection reveals the costly problems with the property.

Safety Clauses

Purchase agreements always come with contingency clauses. There are some clauses that are particularly effective for property flippers.

- *Subject to Inspection.* This is a standard contingency for all purchase agreements – and it is even more so for fixer-upper properties. Though you realize that the home needs repair – hence the reason you are buying it – but there is a difference between renovating the kitchen and rebuilding the foundation. If after your full inspection you find that there are just too many repairs, this clause allows you to negotiate a new purchase price or simply back out of the offer.

- *Subject to Financing.* If you are getting financing, you should be pre-approved *before* submitting an offer, but if for some reason you are suddenly denied the loan, this clause is your ticket out of the agreement.

- *Subject to Appraisal.* If your offer is substantially below what you believe to be the market value, this clause is not necessary. But if you believe you can do a quick flip, you will want to make doubly sure that you are not paying too much.

The fewer contingencies that you have in a purchase agreement, the more likely it is to be accepted. Sellers generally scorn offers that require them to pay the buyer's closing costs. They also rarely accept offers that are contingent on the sale of another property.

Earnest Money Deposits

You can expect to pay some sort of earnest money deposit to prove to the seller that you are a serious buyer. These deposits are always held by a third party and are not released to the seller until closing. The deposit will be applied to the purchase price.

Make sure that your purchase agreement states that the EMD will be paid after the seller's acceptance. If you are writing a lot of offers, you do not want to wrap up thousands of dollars on offers that go nowhere.

The Inspection

The inspection is no doubt the most important part of the purchase process. Of course, before you submit an offer, you are going to want to take your time and inspect the property. Once the offer is accepted, this is where you inspect the property with a fine toothcomb. This leads to being able to prepare an accurate estimate of the renovation work.

Who to Bring

Unless you have a builder's license and years of on-the-job experience as a contractor, I highly recommend that you bring your general contractor with you. Even if you have to pay him for his time, it will be worth every penny. He will no doubt find issues that you may have missed. He will also be able to identify load bearing walls.

You could also hire a home inspector. These inspection professionals will cost between $400 and $600. Unlike your contractor, he or she will be looking for issues that affect either the safety or security of the home. This would include mold identification, infestations, electrical issues, code violations, plumbing problems etc.

Bringing your agent along with you is also a good idea. As your contractor makes suggestions on how to improve the property, your agent will be able to gauge the market's response and how it will affect the market value.

What to Bring

There are a few standard items you will want to bring to an inspection... and a few unusual items. Your contractor will no doubt bring them as well, but better to have two of something than none at all. Here is a list of what I recommend:

- *Camera:* This is a great way to document problems. It also serves as a good memory aid.

- *Measuring Tape:* Yeah, I know you already have one in your glove compartment.

- *Flashlight:* Comes in handy in the crawl spaces, attics and dark corners in the cabinets.

- *Construction Level:* "Is that wall really plumb? Something in that railing just doesn't li ne up. Hand me the level, please."

- *Binoculars:* You could climb up on the roof to inspect the shingles, or you could stand on solid ground and use your binoculars.

- *Marble:* There is no quicker way to see if a floor is level or if the kitchen cabinets were hung straight.

When inspecting a property for the first time, walk through the whole house to get a feel for it. Then start on one floor and slowly go through each room, each closet, each nook and cranny. Write down everything that is out of the ordinary. Take a picture of all of it.

Your inspection needs to cover three basic areas:

- *Layout* - Remember that buyers want an open floor plan. There should be a nice flow of the house - or the potential to create one. You do not want to have to pass through a bedroom to reach another area of the house.

- *Condition* - Look at the carpet, the tile, the paint, the trim. Carefully inspect the electrical, plumbing and heating systems. These can be real expensive items to replace and unfortunately buyers want them but don't especially like to pay you back for fixing them.

- *Potential* - The real money lies in converting an ugly house into a beauty. You need to look behind the hideous carpet, the repulsive paint colors and the completely dated kitchen and envision what you could do with the place. In fact, the uglier the house, the greater the potential to make an easy buck.

When to Run Away

Okay, so we are looking for unappealing, unattractive ugly houses to work our magic on but there are some properties that just are not worth the effort. There are properties that should make you turn tail and run away - well after you invoke your inspection contingency.

- *Mold* - Mold remediation can be very expensive. If a buyer learns there was a serious mold problem it can be a big turn off. If it is just one small spot, be prepared to replace the drywall or flooring in that area. If, however, there is mold in the walls - RUN!

- *Termites* - If you or your inspector suspects an infestation, you should hire a pest control specialists to see how severe it is. Surface termite damage is one thing, but if you find that they have or are attacking structural components – RUN!

- *Foundation Problems.* There is no money in jacking up a house and replacing the whole foundation. Buyers want a level foundation but don't expect them to pay for it. Foundation problems can cause on going issues for the whole house – even after it is fixed. The best idea is just to stay away and leave it to the professionals.

- *Environmental Problems.* The last thing you want is to buy a property that has land contamination. The United States Environmental Protection Agency (EPA) has an interactive website to check for reported contamination.

If after the inspection you find some surprises that are not in your budget, do not think that they are automatically a deal breaker. If you are working with a highly motivated seller with a "handyman special," they may be ready to either fix the problem themselves, adjust the purchase price or credit the cost. If you want to reduce paying income taxes, have them credit the cost rather than lower the price.

Chapter 7

The Quick Flip

At this point we are going to jump into the deep end and show you how to make money flipping properties. We are going to start with the easiest and quickest - the Quick Flip.

Properties that are Good for a Quick Flip

If you want to make money off a quick flip, then you have to find properties at a cheap price. Real estate agents are going to price the properties at market value so it can be a challenge to find super cheap properties in the MLS. Here are a few other suggestions:

- *For Sale by Owner*
- *Highly Motivated Sellers*
  - *Job Transfers*
  - *Retiring Landlords*
  - *Pre-Foreclosures*
- *Transitional Properties*
- *Ugly Properties*

What is a Quick Flip?

These are proper-ties that require few repairs and no rehabs.

The key is to pur-chase these proper-

Change the Look for Cheap

Properties that are superficially ugly have a great potential to earn a quick dollar in exchange for a bottle of bleach and a couple of gallons of paint. If you want to change the look of a house for cheap consider:

- *A Fresh Coat of Paint.* Stick to neutral modern colors.

- *Replace the Fixtures.* Exchange brass for silver, globe lights for ceiling fans and upgrade fixtures to a more modern design.

- *New Hardware.* It is amazing how the look of a house changes with new nobs, pulls, switches and even hinges.

- *Landscaping.* Aim for low maintenance. A few well-placed shrubs and some hardy flowers can do wonders. Lighting also creates a great first impression.

- *A Bright Front Door.* For some reason, buyers love a brightly colored front door. Spray paint it, don't use a brush.

- *Change the Backyard.* Create a backyard that is safe for the kids and is easy to entertain in.

How to Make Money Flipping Without a Rehab

In order to maximize your return, here are a few tips that can help you:

- *Always buy below market.* Surface changes do not change value, they change perception. An appraiser is going to look past the new faucets and the pretty front door and look at the structure and the market – but your buyers are not nearly that objective. You want to buy the property below market and then sell it at the top of the market value.

Reduce your holding period. The quicker you can resell the property, the less holding costs you will pay (less mortgage interest, taxes, insurance, utilities etc.). If you want to really profit off of it, sell it yourself and save yourself the commission. Start advertising for a buyer as soon as you have waived your purchase contingencies. You could even let your buyers pick out the paint colors.

If you really want to keep it easy, find a buyer before you even close on your purchase. If is a non-bank REO, put "and assigns" after your name on the purchase agreement and then simply assign the contract to your new buyers. You get a check for the difference between your purchase price and the sales price to your end buyer – and your end buyer pays the closing costs.

Another option is to do a double close. You close with the seller (the A/B transaction) and then immediately close with your end buyer (the B/C transaction). The funds from the B/C transaction is used to pay off the A/B. Not all title companies are willing to take the risk of floating the A/B transaction. If you can get your end buyer to escrow his funds with the title company before the A/B transaction, then the liability is reduced.

When trying to sell a property yourself, you need to keep every lead you ever find – whether they are interested right now or not. Who knows, they might not like this property but how about the one you are working on 6 months from now.

Chapter 8

The Renovation

Most of your properties are going to be in this category. They will need varying degrees of repairs, renovation or rehabs to maximize their resale value. The renovation takes much more planning and skill, but it can generate a great deal of satisfaction – and money.

How to Find the Property

While there are properties that could benefit from a rehab all over the place, some properties lend themselves to this more than others. Focus your attention on:

- Fixer-Uppers
- Transitional Properties
- Abandoned Homes
- Stalled Construction
- Multi-family Conversion
- Auction Properties
- Divorce

What's the Difference?

Repairs: To restore the property to a good condition.

Renovation: To make the property new or as if new again. To reinvigorate, refresh or revive.

Rehabilitation: To make livable or to

How to Determine Profitability

This is where you are going to need a calculator. Profitability is a combination of purchase price, holding costs, accurate renovation estimates and your desired profit. Here is the formula again as a reminder:

$$(ARV \times .70) - Rehab\ Costs = Maximum\ Allowable\ Offer$$

The Purchase Price

It all starts with the purchase price. If you "accidentally" over pay by 5 to 10% then you are going to have that same amount cut out of your profit when you sell. So, how do you know if you are buying a property for a fair price? Your network is invaluable. It is not just a matter of getting a CMA from your agent but also consulting with your contractor. Sure, the property is worth $185,000 until you find out the roof needs a total replacement.

The Rehab

If you think the price you pay for the property is important, the work estimates can make or break your project. Renovation never goes as smooth as you hope. If you want to play it safe, get your written (remember written) estimates and then add 5% to them. If you can do it for less, great more profit for you! But if things get complicated, you have a cushion.

There are some projects that are vastly more profitable than others. Here are the top 5 renovations in order of demand:

- *Kitchen:* Don't think you have to drop $25K - $50,000 to renovate a kitchen. Resurfacing cabinets keeps the structure (which is usually still good) while giving them an updated and more modern face (which is usually the problem). Consider concrete countertops manufactured to look like granite (for a fraction of the cost and all the durability).

- *Baths:* New flooring, fresh colors and new fixtures can change drab to chic. His and her sinks in the master bathroom are a good seller. Look to tuck a powder room in on the main floor.

- *Open Floor Plan:* Older homes are great fixer-uppers but they tend to be choppy and claustrophobic. Removing a non-load bearing wall to open up the living area can move a 1950's house up into the 21st century.

- *Landscaping and Curb Appeal:* First impressions are important. Keep the yard green and well-trimmed. Clean the siding and the gutters. Paint the front door. Replace the garage door if needed and add some shrubs and flowers.

- *Flooring:* Old ratty flooring really dates a house. Don't just slam something down and call it new. Moving up from vinyl to tile and carpet to wood can move a house up to a new price level if done tastefully.

- *Other Projects*: Other options that buyers are willing to pay for include additional bedrooms and baths along with garage and attic conversions. Master suite additions can dramatically increase the resale value but often do not return the full amount so work closely with your contractor, appraiser and agent.

The After Repair Value

At this point, don't take a shot in the dark. Talk to your contractor about what he recommends and get the estimates in writing. Now take these estimates to your real estate agent. You need to know if spending $15,000 on the kitchen is going pay you back the $15,000 and at least earn you your 20% or $3,000. Your agent will need to do a CMA on the finished product to determine your After Repair Value (AVR).

When you get your ARV, this number is now gospel. The ARV cannot be tweaked, edged up, altered or adjusted. **When you start saying, "Oh don't worry, I'll just ask $5,000 more – we'll get it, I'm sure. Because..." you are treading on very thin ice.** This is the number one reason property flippers fail – they keep changing the ARV on the property. **Don't do it. Change your repairs. Change your profit margin. But do not change the ARV. Trust your agent.**

Do It Yourself vs. Hiring a Contractor

Sure, you've done all sorts of repairs around your house. You even upgraded your own kitchen. You've got '*skilz*'. Unfortunately, just because you know how to use a circular saw and to swing a hammer does not mean that you are an experienced renovation expert. There is a big difference from fixing your own house and remodeling a home you intend to market. We tend to overlook little mistakes but buyer and especially inspectors will not.

Buyers are going to bring through their home inspector. A botched job could cost you the deal and actually lower the price. You also need to consider that some work requires a license and/or permits. In that case, doing the work yourself is definitely not recommended.

Use your contractor for detail specific work where accuracy and perfection are important. Save the "grunt" work for yourself if you are so inclined. There are some other considerations beside your experience and abilities:

- *Do you still have a full-time job?*

- *Do you really want to spend every weekend for 6 months with a hammer, chisel and paint brush?*

- *Can you afford the repairs if you quit your job and focus on this project?*

Contractors are used to working on a deadline, whereas as homeowners commonly tend to procrastinate and put off what they can do tomorrow. Every week that passes is another week that you have to pay holding costs. The quicker you can turn the project over, the quicker you will make your profit. Perhaps you may want to consider leaving the construction to your contractor and become the general manager instead.

How to Manage the Rehab

Time *is* money. Ensuring that all your contractors are getting the work done on schedule will pay off in the end. It take '*skilz*' to schedule all the different contractors and jobs to maximize the time.

There will also be bills to be paid and a budget to scrutinize. You need to keep your contractors and your desire to keep upgrading reigned in on the budget. The minute you exceed market tolerances by upgrading or overbuilding, you are cutting into your profit margin.

Stay organized by creating to-do lists. As you get close to completing the project, create a final punch list of all the little things that perhaps the contractor "over looked."

Chapter 9

Transitional Properties

Transitional properties are perhaps one of the most overlooked gold mines for property flippers. As humans, we resist change. Our eyes dictate utility. We miss opportunities.

For example, an area was recently rezoned from residential to office/service. There is a high traffic road that runs through this new zoned area. On that road are several older residential homes.

One was listed for sale. The asking price is $185,000. It is old and in need of some serious attention but after a little research you find out that the lot itself is worth $75,000. So the value is in the land. Land typically represents 20% of the property value. That means this site could feasibly carry a price of $375,000 if a brand new office building was built on it.

What is a Transitional Property?

A property that is on the verge of being transformed into a new utility such as a residential home that was re-

But what about that old house? It is now a transitional property. The value is no longer in its utility as a residential property but in its *conversion* into an office building.

All you need to do is to change the market perception of the home and change it into a professional office. Take out the features that make this a "home" and create an office atmosphere with a reception area, lunch room and offices. Attorneys, tax consultants, insurance salesmen and real estate companies often buy these types of properties.

Where to Start

Keep track of your local planning and zoning office. Follow their activity. Go to their public meetings. Where are they changing the zoning? Where are areas of new construction? Where are the changes?

Legal Considerations

Transitional properties are often grandfathered in or are considered legally non-conforming. That means that a residential home though under the office zoning does not need to meet the building requirements for a new office building. But... if you start renovating a property, that could all change. So, before you jump in, make sure that you know what you are getting into and what will be required if you alter the utility of the building.

To Renovate or Not to Renovate?

Not all buildings will lend themselves to being renovated. In that case, you may consider buying an appropriately zone lot and moving the structure.

Take the above example, if all the surrounding construction is of a modern strip mall type, having a house in the middle may not have much appeal. Why not buy a residential lot and move the house. The vacant commercial land could be sold for $75,000 and you have a house that could be renovated and sold for full price as well.

Another option is one of simple marketing. FSBO sellers rarely consider transitional value. Grandma and Grampa have lived here for 55 years but they can't stand the traffic anymore. They want out. They never in a million years thought that the land they paid $2,500 for 55 years ago would be worth $75,000. They only think of it as a home. You pick up the property for $110,000 and immediately turn around and sell it to another rehabber for $150,000 and pocket $40,000 tomorrow.

Chapter 10

How to Sell the Finished Product

While you are upgrading and renovating the property, you only have money going out. Now it is time to get some money coming in. The time has come to reap the rewards from all your hard work.

Selling With an Agent vs. Selling On Your Own

Buying a property with the help of your real estate agent is a no-brainer. Since the seller pays their commission, their services are free to you. When it comes to selling, however, their services, experience and assistance will cost you quite a bit.

Paying commission is a significant expense to factor into your profitability equation. When you multiplied your ARV by .70, the commission is automatically figured in as part of your 30% profit margin. Typically real estate agents will charge 5-7% of the sales price. On a $250,000 sale, you are looking between $12,500 and $17,500. If you have a good real estate agent, however, it is totally worth it.

Your agent will do more than simply find you a buyer. They foot the cost for the marketing of your property. They take the time to show all interested parties the home. They will negotiate with buyers and their agents to get you the highest price possible. They will work with the agency that is handling the closing to make sure everything is completed. If there are any complications in any of these areas, your agent will step up to the plate and work to resolve them.

This frees up your time to focus on finding your next investment. You need to weigh whether you have the resources and the skills necessary to take their place if you decide to go it alone. Real estate transactions are rarely cut and dried, the potential for a lawsuit from a dissatisfied buyer is always present. Having a licensed agent is a prime way to reduce the likelihood of that happening.

That being said, I would recommend that for your first couple of properties, you use the services of an agent. It will help prepare you for the realities of selling the property, if you decide to go at it alone down the road.

How to Attract Buyers

The quicker you can locate the buyer the better. You want them to pick your home over the others that are competing against you. Here are some suggestions that will make your property stand out above the crowd.

Staging

Buyers need a little encouragement to envision how the home will look when furnished. Empty rooms do little to spur imagination.

It has been proven that a home which has been well staged sells for more than if the home was sold vacant – even though the buyer keeps none of the furnishings.

You have three basic options: Professional stagers, rent-to-own companies and the do-it-yourself option. Professional stagers are worth the cost if you are selling a mid-to-high range home. Another option is to rent a living room and master bedroom set from a rental company and then return it when the house sells. If you need to reduce costs and are looking for the minimum, put up some neutral curtains and set out some healthy house plants.

Open Houses

Having an open house is a great way to show the community what you have done to improve the property. Display before and after photos. Make sure you set out some flyers and business cards. You just may get a good referral out of it.

Lease Options and Land Contracts

Quite a few buyers have decent credit but lack the down payment necessary to get a loan. If after a though background check and credit report, you deem them to be low risk, consider selling the home on a lease option or land contract. Though this will lock up your capital for a year or two, the additional payments and interest can increase your return. The lease option will entail two documents - one for the lease and the other for the purchase. The renter will pay market rent plus a monthly payment for the future purchase of the house. If they back out of the lease option, all payments are non-refundable.

Another option is to sell the property on a land contract. The down payment is less (generally less than 10%) but the interest rate is higher than conventional loans. After three to five years, the buyer must pay off the loan freeing up your capital.

Chapter 11

Challenges to Property Flipping

Property flipping is a very profitable business for those who are willing to work hard, stick to a budget and invest in the right properties. There are, however, some challenges that can make this business a risky and often stressful one. Here are the top five challenges and how to get around them:

1. Flipping is not always profitable.

It is very difficult to make money flipping properties when price appreciation slows or reverses. Property flippers expect property values to have increased during the holding period which adds to their bottom line.

In strong markets, a lack of discounted homes and foreclosure deals can reduce the supply and increase competition among flippers. Property flipping in higher-priced markets such as San Francisco, Seattle, Denver, New York City and Los Angeles can be a real challenge since it costs so much to get the property in the first place.

Flippers who do this full-time often run into cash flow problems. While the property is under construction, it is constant money going out. It can take six months of renovation bills in order to see any income. Flippers need to stay on top of the market and have a reasonable plan to pay for the repairs.

2. Lack of Experience

Poor quality renovations and repairs can actually pull down the value of the home as buyers see it more as a liability than an upgrade. Make sure you use your contractor where it counts, it will be worth the money spent.

3. Lengthy Holding Period

Flippers who drag their feet during the renovation period will see rising holding costs which will slowly eat away at their profits. In addition, there are periods during the year where buyers are few and far between. Time your construction to fall during the slow times such as November - February and then put the home on the market as buyers come out of hibernation.

4. Tax Implications

Because you will sell the property within the first year of ownership, you will not have to pay capital gains tax, but the profit you make off the sale will be taxed as ordinary income. Unless your tax advisor or accountant helps you to set up the appropriate corporation, it will be taxed as self-employment income. When it comes to corporations, look into an S-Corp rather than a LLC. S-Corps offer more tax advantages and legal protections than LLCs. So, before you go out and spend all your profits, make sure you set aside around 25% to pay your taxes... and make an appointment to consult with your CPA.

5. The ARV is Constantly Changing

More than any other challenge, this one here causes the death of a property flipper more than any other. Flippers who always think they can sell the property for a little more will quickly find out that the market is not that gullible. Get a reliable ARV and stick to it, no matter what.

Chapter 12

10 Tips to Make the Most Money Flipping Houses

Would you like to know a few of the trade secrets? Well I am going to let you in on a few tips I have picked up over the years. Implementing these points will reduce risk and stress and increase profits.

1. Do not take on more risk than you can bear.

2. Choose the best investment, not the first property.

3. Correctly calculate your holding costs.

4. Do not overbuild.

5. Do not run out of money and stall the project.

6. Watch your time vs. money. If it takes you 6 months of working full-time on the rehab to make $5,000 profit, you are only earning $5.20 an hour.

7. Be patient. Professionals take their time and wait for the right property. Novices rush out and buy the first fixer-upper they find and hire the cheapest contractor.

8. Try to sell the house yourself and save the commission.

9. Develop a system. Create a step-by-step process. Use the same suppliers, the same materials, the same paint colors and the same timeline where possible. Not only will it simplify the process and reduce stress but it will make it much easier to estimate renovation costs.

10. Always estimate more for repairs than what you think. Repairs frequently cost more than estimated and unforeseen repairs always show up, so be prepared from the start.

And… If you really want to maximize your return, consider living in the property while renovating. In this way you are always on-site and can work longer and harder on a project. Meanwhile, your holding costs are your living expenses. While this may work well for singles, I do not recommend it for newlyweds or families with children – for obvious reasons.

How to Get Started

I hope this book has helped you to understand the ins and outs of property flipping. If you dream of working for yourself and enjoy working with your hands and have the skills to boot, this can be a truly rewarding line of work – and a profitable one at that.

Now it comes to the point getting it off the paper and into reality. If you are ready to get started, here is where you should begin:

1. Figure out your financing.

    a. Save for a down payment.

    b. Get pre-approved.

    c. Figure out how to pay for the repairs.

2. Partner with a real estate agent.

3. Find a contractor.

4. Find 20 houses.

   a. MLS

   b. Notice of Defaults

   c. Non-listed run down properties

   d. FSBOs

5. Analyze them all.

   a. Analyze the property

   b. Study the market

   c. Determine buyer's wants and needs.

6. Make an offer on the best options.

7. After the closing, start the work.

   a. Stay on budget

   b. Watch your costs vs. ARV

   c. Do the highest quality work possible.

8. While in the end stages of construction, market the property.

9. Sell the property.

10. Repeat from Step 4.

It all starts with one good property. Once that is rehabbed and sold, the profits can be slid over into the next investment and then the business grows, the systems improve and the return on your investments compound. So just don't sit there, go for it!

Conclusion

This guide will serve you well along your journey. I hope that you took notes and you are ready to move forward with your house flipping goals. Flipping houses entails a lot of curve balls along the way. It's important that you understand that you will never be 100% prepared or ready for every obstacle that you encounter.

If flipping houses is something that you have been contemplating for some time now, commit to a flip. Start small and work your way up. The lessons you learn along the way will be invaluable.

Could I ask you one favor? Could you please leave me a review? I would be forever grateful. If you are interested in other real estate endeavors here is a list of some of my other books:

Wholesaling Real Estate: A beginners Guide

Rental Property Investing for the Rest of Us: The Beginners Guide to Successful Rental Property Investing

Becoming a Real Estate Agent: A Comprehensive Guide on How to Become a Real Estate Agent

www.ingramcontent.com/pod-product-compliance
Lightning Source LLC
Chambersburg PA
CBHW070932180526
45168CB00003B/1048